Celebrating CHRIST WITH Youth-Led WORShip

A 4-week course to help teenagers
create and lead celebrations of Jesus' life

by Stephen Parolini

Group®

Loveland, Colorado

Group®

Celebrating Christ With Youth-Led Worship
Copyright © 1994 Group Publishing, Inc.

First Printing

Credits
Edited by Michael Warden
Cover designed by Liz Howe and Amy Bryant

ISBN 1-55945-410-5
Printed in the United States of America

Session 6

HOT-THOT

"If any of you lacks wisdom, he should ask God, who gives generously to all without finding fault, and it will be given to him."

James 1:5

The Wisdom File:

Case # Proverbs 16:7 and 29:11

My investigation this week involves three suspects:

1. A hardened criminal in murder, arson, stealing, cheating, lying— well, his police record goes on and on. His name is Satan.

2. A typical young girl named Jane.

3. Her typical twin sister Joan.

I witnessed the following incident. Satan approached Jane and said:

HEY, JANE! DID YOU HEAR THE TERRIBLE GOSSIP SAM SNORKLE IS SPREADING ABOUT YOU? GO PUNCH HIM IN THE SNOUT!

GRRR!

Which she did. It was horrible!

POW!

Then Satan approached sister Joan and said:

?

HEY, JOAN! DID YOU HEAR THE TERRIBLE GOSSIP SAM SNORKLE IS SPREADING ABOUT YOU? GO PUNCH HIM IN THE SNOUT!

NO! THE BIBLE SAYS, "A FOOL GIVES FULL VENT TO HIS ANGER, BUT A WISE MAN KEEPS HIMSELF UNDER CONTROL." PROVERBS 29:11, NIV.

"WHEN A MAN'S WAYS ARE PLEASING TO THE LORD, HE MAKES EVEN HIS ENEMIES TO BE AT PEACE WITH HIM." PROVERB 16:7, NASB. THAT'S WHAT THE BIBLE SAYS AND THAT'S WHAT I'M GONNA DO!

CURSES! FOILED AGAIN!

Sleuth's comment:

Jane and Joan are alike in many ways. Both look the same, like the same things, and do many of the same things. But there is ONE IMPORTANT EXCEPTION: Joan is wise. She follows the Bible. She lets God be her guide.

Seems to me everyone should be like Joan!

DAILY NUGGETS Wisdom from God's Word for you to read each day.

Day 1 Read 1 Corinthians 1:18. What is considered foolish by the world?

Day 2 1 Corinthians 1:19-25. What do these verses tell you about man's way of thinking compared to God's?

Day 3 Matthew 7:24-27. Think of an illustration from your everyday life that is similar to this classic example of a fool and a wise man.

Day 4 Luke 12:13-21. In your Bible, circle the sentences or phrases that demonstrate the following steps to foolishness: 1. A fool does not recognize what life consists of. 2. A fool thinks he controls his own destiny. 3. A fool does not take God into consideration.

Day 5 2 Timothy 3:15. According to this verse where can you get the wisdom that leads to salvation?

Day 6 Proverbs 3:5,6. Rewrite this in your own words.

Describe-a-Fool*

* The word *fool* in the Scripture suggests conceit and pride, not mental inferiority—in other words, the guy is not a dummy!

How does this guy deceive himself?
Galatians 6:3

What a fool does in conversation:
Proverbs 29:9,11

What a fool mocks or laughs at:
Proverbs 14:9

What a fool despises:
Proverbs 1:7

What the fool says in his heart:
Psalm 14:1

What are the by-products of worldly wisdom or foolishness?
James 3:13-16

How did this guy become a fool?
Romans 1:21

List the ways a fool lives:
Titus 3:3

This joker thinks he's standing. What might happen to him?
1 Corinthians 10:12

Words of Wisdom

Where does true wisdom come from?
Proverbs 2:6,7

Heavenly wisdom is:
James 3:17

God will direct your path if:
Proverbs 3:5,6

"If any of you lacks wisdom, he should ask God, who gives generously to all without finding fault, and it will be given to him."
James 1:5

If you really care about yourself what will you do?
Proverbs 19:8

If you lack wisdom in life you should:
James 1:5

What should you do to be able to withstand troubles?
Matthew 7:24-29

What happens to this guy's enemies when he does what is pleasing to the Lord?
Proverbs 16:7

Don't Fool Yourself

Based on the Scriptures you've read, check the box that best describes you.

☐ I tend to fool myself into thinking that people or things will make me happy.

☐ I want to be wise—but I do act foolishly about certain things.

☐ I feel that I'm growing in wisdom all the time.

☐ Sometimes I'm so wise I surprise myself.
Other times—well, I surprise myself then too.

Write down one area in which you lean toward foolishness. For example: Attitudes at home or school, self-control of your mouth, eyes, hands, etc.

How about asking God to give you His wisdom in dealing with your problem area? (Make a written request.)

CONTENTS

Lesson 1	9

Celebrating Christ

Teenagers will lead the congregation in celebrating Jesus' birth.

Lesson 2	18

Jesus, the Master Teacher

Teenagers will lead the congregation in celebrating Jesus' teaching ministry.

Lesson 3	24

Jesus, Our Savior

Teenagers will lead the congregation in celebrating Jesus' role as Savior.

Lesson 4	30

Jesus Will Return

Teenagers will lead the congregation in celebrating the promise of Jesus' return.

Bonus Ideas	35

Introduction
CELEBRATING CHRIST WITH YOUTH-LED WORSHIP

What do teenagers celebrate? Football victories. Saving enough money for a ski trip. Getting a perfect score on a history test. Finding a new boyfriend or girlfriend. A birthday.

Kids today love to celebrate. And why not? With all the problems in their world, teenagers need to focus on something good. So let's give teenagers something, or rather *someone*, wonderful to celebrate—Jesus.

In the next four weeks your teenagers will create and lead celebrations of Jesus' birth, his teaching ministry, his death and resurrection, and his promise to return.

Plus, your church will reap the benefits of these celebrations.

Each week, as kids explore one aspect of Jesus' life, they'll discover more about Christ and grow closer to him. Then they'll put their creativity into producing a celebration the whole church can enjoy. This course provides a great way for kids to involve themselves in the life of your church.

And in the process, through study and planning, kids will build relationships with Christ and with each other.

Nothing is more exciting to a church than the contagious energy young people can bring to an otherwise predictable worship service. Use this course to give your congregation four weeks of celebrating the person who called them together in the first place—Jesus Christ.

COURSE OBJECTIVES

By the end of this course, your students will
- celebrate Jesus' birth, teaching ministry, death and resurrection, and promise to return;
- explore different perspectives on Jesus' birth;
- discover how Jesus taught with authority;
- learn what Jesus' death and resurrection mean to them; and
- discover the hope in Jesus' promise to return.

THIS COURSE AT A GLANCE

Before you dive into the lessons, familiarize yourself with each lesson aim. Then read the Scripture passages.
- Study them as a background to the lessons.
- Use them as a basis for your personal devotions.
- Think about how they relate to kids' circumstances today.

Lesson 1: CELEBRATING CHRIST
Lesson Aim: Teenagers will lead the congregation in celebrating Jesus' birth.
Bible Basis: Isaiah 9:1-7.

Lesson 2: JESUS, THE MASTER TEACHER
Lesson Aim: Teenagers will lead the congregation in celebrating Jesus' teaching ministry.
Bible Basis: Mark 1:21-22.

Lesson 3: JESUS, OUR SAVIOR
Lesson Aim: Teenagers will lead the congregation in celebrating Jesus' role as Savior.
Bible Basis: Mark 15:21-39; 16:1-6.

Lesson 4: JESUS WILL RETURN
Lesson Aim: Teenagers will lead the congregation in celebrating the promise of Jesus' return.
Bible Basis: Matthew 28:20b; John 14:1-3; 1 Thessalonians 4:13-18; and Revelation 22:20.

HOW TO USE THIS COURSE

PROJECTS WITH A PURPOSE ™ for Youth Ministry

Think back on an important lesson you've learned in life. Did you learn it by reading about it? from hearing a lecture about it?

Chances are, the most important lessons you've learned came from something you experienced. That's what active learning is—learning by doing. And active learning is a key element in Group's new Projects With a Purpose™ courses.

Active learning leads students in doing things that help them understand important principles, messages, and ideas. It's a discovery process that helps kids internalize what they learn.

Research about active learning indicates that maximum learning results when students are involved in direct, purposeful experiences. With that in mind, each Projects With a Purpose course gives teachers tools to facilitate some sort of project that results in direct, purposeful experiences for teenagers. Projects, experiences, and immersion into real-life faith action characterize this curriculum. Each course produces a tangible result. You'll find plenty of helpful hints that'll make this course easy for you to teach and meaningful to your students.

Projects With a Purpose takes learning to a new level—giving teenagers an opportunity to discover something significant about their faith. And kids learn the important skills of working together, sharing one another's troubles, and supporting each other in love.

Projects With a Purpose offers a fun, alternative way for teenagers to put their faith in action. Use it today to involve your kids in Christian growth experiences they'll remember for a lifetime.

Before the 4-Week Course

■ Read the Introduction, the Course Objectives, and This Course at a Glance.

■ Determine when you'll use this course. Projects With a Purpose works well in Sunday school classes, midweek meetings, home Bible studies, confirmation classes, youth groups, special interest groups, leadership groups, retreats, camps, or any time you want to help teenagers discover more about their faith.

■ Decide how you'll publicize the course using the clip art on the Publicity Page (p. 8). Prepare fliers, newsletter articles, and posters as needed.

■ Look at the Bonus Ideas (p. 35) and decide which ones you'll use.

Before Each Lesson

Read the opening statements, Objectives, and Bible Basis for the lesson. The Bible Basis focuses on a key biblical theme for the activity, experience, or Bible study portion of the lesson.

Gather necessary supplies from This Lesson at a Glance.

Read each section of the lesson. Adjust as necessary for your class size and meeting room.

Helpful Hints

■ The approximate minutes listed give you an idea of how long each activity will take. Each lesson in a Projects With a Purpose course is designed to fill an hour-long time slot. Some lessons may require work outside of class, depending on the project for the course. You might also consider restructuring your class time, if possible, to allow more time to complete projects.

The answers given after discussion questions are responses your students *might* give. They aren't the only answers or the "right" answers. If needed, use them to spark discussion. Kids won't always say what you wish they'd say. That's why some of the responses given are negative or controversial. If someone responds negatively, don't be shocked. Accept the person and use the opportunity to explore other angles of the issue.

■ If you see you're going to have extra time, do an activity or two from the "If You Still Have Time..." section at the end of each lesson, or from the Bonus Ideas (p. 35).

■ Dive into the activities with the kids. Don't be a spectator. The experience will be more successful and rewarding for both you and your students when you play an active role.

■ Have fun with the lessons as you lead your teenagers. Remember, it was Jesus who encouraged us to become "like little children." Besides, how often do your kids get *permission* to express their childlike qualities?

■ Be prepared for surprises. In Projects With a Purpose Bible curriculum lessons, you don't always know which way the lesson will go. Much of your job will be directing kids to stay on task, rather than leading specific activities. As facilitator, you'll be helping kids make their own faith discoveries, rather than directing the results of a specific activity.

■ Encourage new leaders to participate in teaching this course. Projects With a Purpose offers an exciting way to give new volunteers a hands-on look at the positive impact youth ministry can have on teenagers.

■ Rely on the Holy Spirit to help you. Remember, only God can give true spiritual insight. Concentrate on your role as the facilitator and trust the Holy Spirit to work in the hearts of your kids.

You Can Do It!

Because Projects With a Purpose is a different approach to Christian education, leading the lessons might seem a bit scary at first.

That's OK. In fact, it's normal to be a little nervous about a new teaching method. Innovation often requires a risk for the teacher. But hang in there. With the Holy Spirit's guidance and your own desire to make these lessons succeed, great things will happen in your kids' lives.

Grab your teenagers' attention! Photocopy this page, then cut out and paste the clip art of your choice in your church bulletin or newsletter to advertise this course on celebrating Christ. Or photocopy and use the ready-made flier as a bulletin insert. Permission to photocopy this clip art is granted for local church use.

Splash the clip art on posters, fliers, or even postcards! Just add the vital details: the date and time the course begins and where you'll meet.

It's that simple.

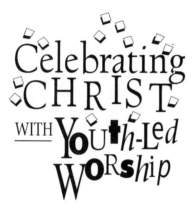

Come to ....

On ....

At ....

Help us plan and lead four celebrations of Jesus' life for the whole church!

A 4-week youth project to creatively celebrate what Jesus has done for us

Celebrating Christ

Teenagers learn a lot about Jesus at church. If they've been raised in the church, kids have probably heard more times than they can remember that Jesus died for their sins. But they specifically celebrate Christ only a couple of times a year—Easter and Christmas.

Kids can celebrate their Lord all year round. Part of the fun of this course is to celebrate Jesus' life during other times of the year! This lesson introduces a series of four projects to help teenagers celebrate Christ with the whole church.

Teenagers will lead the congregation in celebrating Jesus' birth.

Students will
■ define the purpose of the course,
■ explore perspectives on Jesus' birth, and
■ invite the church to participate in their celebration of Jesus' birth.

Look up the following key Bible passage. Then read the background paragraphs to see how the passage relates to your teenagers. This Scripture will be explored during the Bible study portion of this lesson.

Isaiah 9:1-7 describes Isaiah's vision of a coming Messiah.

When Isaiah wrote this passage, Judah was faced with troubles from neighboring countries. King Ahaz looked to Assyria for protection, even though Isaiah correctly predicted the fall of the northern tribes of Israel to the Assyrians. Ahaz's son, Hezekiah, instituted spiritual reforms but looked to a soon-to-be-fallen Egypt for help with foreign affairs.

In the midst of this turmoil, Isaiah predicts the coming of the Messiah. What must these people have thought of Isaiah's prediction? Were they hopeful? Or did they fall into deeper despair as they watched the already powerful Assyrians grow even more powerful? Only in retrospect can we fathom the incredible power of Isaiah's message of a coming Messiah.

Teenagers today face many troubles and times of uncertainty. Like the God-fearing people of Isaiah's time, they long to

LESSON AIM

OBJECTIVES

BIBLE BASIS

ISAIAH 9:1-7

experience the hope of a coming Messiah—and the promise of justice. Through this lesson kids will explore the significance of Jesus' birth for their lives. And they'll come to see Jesus as someone who brings hope to the hopeless.

THIS LESSON AT A GLANCE

Section	Minutes	What Students Will Do	Supplies
Introduction	up to 10	**Celebrating Christ**—Define the purpose of this course and introduce themselves.	
Bible Study	up to 10	**Jesus Is Born**—Read Isaiah 9:1-7 and Luke 1:26-33 and explore different perspectives on Jesus' birth.	Bibles
Project Work	up to 30	**Celebrating Jesus' Birth**—Prepare for and invite church members to participate in their celebration of Jesus' birth.	Banner supplies, birthday decorations, "Celebration Plan—Week One" handouts (p. 15), pencils
	up to 15	**Coming Soon**—Plan the coming week's celebration activity.	"Celebration Plan—Week Two" handouts (p. 16), pencils
Closing	up to 10	**The Baby's Cry**—Listen to the cry of a baby and imagine what it would've been like to see Jesus as a baby.	Cassette recording of a baby crying, cassette player

The Lesson

Celebrating Christ
(up to 10 minutes)

Welcome students to the class. Say: **Today we're going to begin a four-week celebration of Jesus Christ. But instead of typical activities and discussions, we're going to create innovative ways to celebrate Jesus' life with the whole congregation.**

Open with prayer.

Form groups of no more than five. Say: **Beginning with the person who has the brightest colored shoes, complete the following sentence in your group: "My favorite Bible story about Jesus is..."**

After the first person tells his or her favorite story, have groups continue clockwise until each person has spoken.

Then call everyone together and ask:

■ **Why did you choose your particular story?** (I like the fact that Jesus loved us enough to die for us; I'm intrigued by Jesus' power.)

■ **What does this activity say about the people in our group?** (We're a diverse group; many of us like the same stories.)

Say: **We all bring different perspectives and interests to this class. As we work together on ways to celebrate Christ, let's respect those differences and take advantage of each other's interests. Let's also remember to have fun.**

Jesus Is Born

(up to 10 minutes)

Say: **One of the most significant events in our lives happened 2,000 years ago—Jesus' birth. And no celebration of Christ would be complete without thanking God for sending Jesus in the first place. To begin our series of celebrations, let's explore the Scriptures and what they say about this miracle birth.**

Form groups of no more than four. Have each group member choose one of the following time periods: when Jesus was born, when Jesus was teaching the disciples, immediately after Jesus ascended into heaven, and today.

Have kids read Isaiah 9:1-7 and Luke 1:26-33 and explore, from the perspective of their assigned time periods, the significance of Jesus' birth. For example, someone from the time "when Jesus was born" might think the birth of this baby was nothing special, or people who studied the Scriptures might wonder if this is the promised Messiah written about in Isaiah. Have kids discuss their ideas in their groups, then have volunteers share their insights with the class. Ask:

■ **Why do we celebrate Jesus' birth so joyously?** (Because it represents God reaching down to us; because it's a tradition; because we want to remember God's Son.)

■ **How is the way the people in Isaiah's time looked forward to a Messiah like the way we look forward to Christmas?** (I don't look forward to Christmas—it's a depressing time for me; we anticipate the happiness of Christ's birth, just as the people of Isaiah's time looked forward to a time of happiness instead of oppression.)

■ **How do you think the people of Isaiah's time would have responded if God had announced that a baby born to a virgin was going to be their Messiah?** (They wouldn't have believed God; they'd be skeptical.)

Say: **When Isaiah prophesied about the Messiah, the people were longing for someone to enter their world and make things right. But the Jews didn't think that their Messiah would be a suffering servant. And they certainly didn't expect that their "knight in shining armor" would be crucified. Many people still don't understand why God chose to become a human, to suffer pain and despair, and to ultimately die on the cross for us.**

These next four weeks, as we become intimately involved in the person of Jesus, let's remove our

BIBLE STUDY

PROJECT WORK

Teacher Tip

If you're meeting outside of the regular Christian education hour, revise your opening statements to reflect the time you'll actually present the first celebration. For example, if you're meeting during the week, have kids plan to present their first celebration just before or after your next scheduled worship service.

Teacher Tip

If your class chooses one large celebration, you may want to ask the smaller groups to take on specific responsibilities for the celebration. For example, some kids might want to draw a banner, while others might be happier singing in front of the church.

expectations and meet Jesus for who he is. And let's prepare to walk the road with him as we learn from our Bible studies and celebrations.

Celebrating Jesus' Birth

(up to 30 minutes)

Say: **The goal of these next four weeks is to celebrate Jesus' life and what he's done for us. We'll begin by celebrating Jesus' birth with the whole church immediately following class time.**

Form groups of no more than six and give each group a "Celebration Plan—Week One" handout (p. 15) and a pencil. Have groups use the handout to brainstorm ways they can celebrate Jesus' birth with the whole church. Refer kids to the "Idea Sparks" box on the handout for a few starter ideas, but encourage them to use their own creativity.

To help with the brainstorming, bring out banner supplies (butcher paper, markers, construction paper, scissors, glue), birthday decorations, and other supplies that might give kids celebration ideas. You'll need to know what other kinds of supplies are available in your church, such as scrap cloth, costumes, stage props, and so on.

Give groups five to 10 minutes to brainstorm and complete steps one, two, and three on the handout.

Have groups each explain their best celebration idea to the class. Then you may choose to vote on one idea, or have groups do different ideas. If you choose more than one idea, form groups to do each idea (and complete steps four and five on the handout). If you choose to do only one idea, form small groups of no more than four to brainstorm the details of the idea (steps four and five on the handout). Have those groups pool the ideas and choose the best way to proceed.

After determining which celebration kids want to do, help them choose what they'll do to make the celebration a success. Refer to the "Responsibilities" box on the "Celebration Plan—Week One" handout to help kids think about different ways to be involved in the celebration.

When kids have each chosen a responsibility for the celebration, have them begin preparing. To help things go smoothly, assign a leader for each area of responsibility required by the celebration (areas of responsibility include prop research, banner or sign creation, celebration presentation, publicity, and volunteer solicitation).

If kids need to track down supplies, send them out in small groups, but be sure they return to your classroom in time to make plans for the coming week's celebration (you'll need 10 to 15 minutes for this) and for the closing activity (another ten minutes).

For this first celebration, have kids also create an advertisement about the four-week-course theme so congregation members will understand what the "big party" is all about. For example, a simple advertisement might be a poster that says, "Join us during the next four weeks as we celebrate Christ. Look for a new celebration next week!" Kids can use this same notice in the coming weeks, or they can create a new advertisement each week.

Coming Soon
(up to 15 minutes)

When kids are prepared for their first celebration, form groups of no more than six to brainstorm ideas for next week's celebration activity. Have groups use the "Celebration Plan—Week Two" handout (p. 16) to spark new ideas on the theme of Jesus, the master teacher. Encourage kids to vary their celebrations so church members won't know what to expect. For example, kids might lead an impromptu party one week and a sing-along the next time.

After about five or 10 minutes, have groups report what they came up with. Then determine which ideas you'll actually use. If kids need to prepare for the coming week's celebration outside of class time, determine what they must do. For example, if your celebration requires food, kids would need volunteers to make or bring food.

If you don't have time to plan for next week's celebration, that's OK. You can use the first part of next week's class to finalize your planning.

Collect the "Celebration Plan—Week Two" handouts for use in next week's lesson. Kids will begin next week's lesson by reviewing their plans for the day's celebration.

Table Talk

The "Table Talk" activity in this course helps teenagers celebrate Christ with their families. If you choose to use the "Table Talk" activity, this is a good time to show students the "Table Talk" handout (p. 17). Ask them to spend time with their parents completing it.

Before kids leave, give them each the "Table Talk" handout to take home or tell them you'll be sending it to their parents. Tell kids to be prepared to report next week on their experiences with the handout.

The Baby's Cry
(up to 10 minutes)

About ten minutes before the class ends, call kids together and have them form pairs. Play a cassette of a crying baby softly in the background and have pairs briefly discuss the following questions:

■ **How does the sound of a crying baby make you feel about Jesus' birth?** (I'm reminded that Jesus was born as a

Teacher Tip

If you have a limited amount of class time to prepare and plan for the celebration, try one of these alternative structures:

■ Form two groups, one to work on today's celebration and one to prepare next week's celebration. For the actual celebration, all the kids could be involved (as long as it is presented after class time).

■ Plan to meet outside of class time to plan the next week's celebration. Have kids use out-of-class time to make plans for the celebration and collect needed supplies.

CLOSING

human; I wonder if Jesus ever cried as a baby; I wonder how God felt as he looked upon the baby Jesus.)

■ **What would it have been like to live when Jesus was born?** (It would've been exciting; I wouldn't have known what to say; I'd be in awe.)

Say: **As we prepare to present our first celebration of Christ, let's spend a moment in prayer, thanking God for the unique individuals here and their great ideas.**

Have teenagers each pray out loud, thanking God specifically for their partner by praying, "Thanks for (name). I'm glad he (or she) was born because..." After the prayer, thank students for attending. Then join them in final preparations for today's celebration. Alert the pastoral staff of the celebration ideas you'll be using.

Make a note of any preparations you'll need to make in the coming week for next week's celebration.

If You Still Have Time...

Giving Gifts—Since we celebrate Jesus' birth each year by the giving of gifts, have kids each describe one gift they'll give to Jesus this year. Encourage kids to think of gifts that relate to their spiritual lives such as "I'll give more time to reading the Bible" or "I'll tell a friend about my faith."

The Prophecies—Have teenagers form groups of no more than four. Have each group read one or more of the following passages: Isaiah 2:4; 53:1-12; and 61:1-3. Ask kids to discuss how these prophecies about the Messiah might have been accepted in Isaiah's time. Then have kids explore how these prophecies apply to Jesus today.

CELEBRATION PLAN—WEEK ONE

Use this as a guide for choosing and preparing your celebration activity for week one's theme of celebrating Jesus' birth. (Read Isaiah 9:1-7 and Luke 1:26-33.) For more writing room, use the other side of this handout.

Step 1—

Brainstorm tons of celebration ideas about Jesus' birth. Use the "Idea Sparks" below to get you going. The celebration must involve everyone in the group (or the class) and must be do-able with easily available supplies (ask your teacher about available supplies). List your ideas on the back of this handout.

Step 2—

OK, you've thought of lots of ideas. Now choose your favorite. This is the one idea you'll expand further with specific plans, so choose wisely. Describe that idea briefly below:

Step 3—

This celebration's most important goal is for people to experience the joy of Jesus' birth. How well does your idea meet this goal? (If you have a hard time answering this question, you may need to rethink your celebration idea.) Write down why your idea really meets this goal. Wait for further instructions from your teacher.

Responsibilities

Behind the scenes:
- drawing
- coloring
- creating posters
- writing slogans
- collecting supplies
- organizing prop creation
- doing publicity
- soliciting volunteers

In the public eye:
- singing
- speaking
- performing a skit
- leading the congregation
- making announcements

Step 4—

So you're ready to plan a specific celebration? Think about what kinds of responsibilities people will have. Refer to the "Responsibilities" in the box for suggestions. Then list who's responsible for what. Write on the back of your handout, if necessary.

Step 5—

How long will this celebration be? When will you present it? Remember, the celebration must involve the congregation in some way. List details on the back of this handout.

Here are a few starter ideas to get the brainstorming going for this week's celebration:
- Throw a birthday party for Jesus after worship.
- Create one or more "Jesus is born!" or "It's a boy!" birthday banners and parade them around the sanctuary during worship.
- Write new words to "Happy Birthday" that describe the joy of Jesus' birth (and sing it during or after worship).
- Create a cheer or poem about the joy of Jesus' birth.
- Use posters, masks, banners, candles, or other props to celebrate Jesus' birth in a silent manner (or through mime).

CELEBRATION PLAN—WEEK TWO

Use this as a guide for choosing and preparing your celebration activity for this week's theme of celebrating Jesus, the master teacher. (Read Mark 1:21-22; John 3:2; 7:16-17; and 14:23-24.) For more writing room, use the other side of this handout.

Step 1—

Brainstorm tons of celebration ideas for the next lesson, "Jesus, the Master Teacher." Use the "Idea Sparks" below to get you going. The celebration must involve everyone in the group (or the class) and must be do-able with easily available supplies (ask your teacher about available supplies). List your ideas on the back of this handout:

Step 2—

OK, you've thought of lots of ideas. Now choose your favorite. This is the one idea you'll expand further with specific plans, so choose wisely. Describe that idea briefly below:

Step 3—

This celebration's most important goal is for people to be filled with joy and thanksgiving for Jesus' ability to teach us. How well does your idea meet this goal? (If you have a hard time answering this question, you may need to rethink your celebration idea.) Write down why your idea really meets this goal. Wait for further instructions.

Step 4—

So you're ready to plan a specific celebration? Think about what kinds of responsibilities people will have. Refer to the "Responsibilities" in the box for suggestions. Then list who's responsible for what. Write on the back of your handout, if necessary.

Step 5—

How long will this celebration be? When will you present it? Remember, the celebration must involve the congregation in some way. List details on the back of this handout.

Responsibilities

Behind the scenes:
- drawing
- coloring
- creating posters
- writing slogans
- collecting supplies
- organizing prop creation
- doing publicity
- soliciting volunteers

In the public eye:
- singing
- speaking
- performing a skit
- leading the congregation
- making announcements

IDEA SPARKS

Here are a few starter ideas to get the brainstorming going for week two's celebration:
- Create a mural depicting some of Jesus' greatest lessons.
- Write a responsive reading for the whole church that describes Jesus, the teacher.
- Have some people act out scenes of Jesus teaching the disciples, while others narrate.
- Acknowledge the teachers in your church for their efforts and ask God to give them teaching skills like Jesus.
- Invite congregation members to tell about their favorite lessons from Jesus' teaching.
- Create a balloon banner by connecting helium balloons side by side. On each balloon list Scripture passages that illustrate Jesus' greatest teachings.

Table Talk

To the Parent: We're involved in a project at church called *Celebrating Christ With Youth-Led Worship.* Students are preparing celebrations of Jesus' birth, friendship, death, and resurrection for the next few weeks. We'd like you and your teenager to spend some time celebrating what Christ has done in your lives. Use this "Table Talk" page to help you do that.

Parent

■ What intrigued you most about Jesus when you were a teenager?
■ What significance did Jesus' birth have at your Christmas celebrations when you were a teenager?
■ How have your views about Jesus changed over the years?
■ How has your family celebrated Christmas traditions?

Teenager

■ What about Jesus' life is most difficult for you to understand?
■ How do Jesus' teachings affect your daily life?
■ How would you describe your relationship with Jesus today, compared to your relationship five years ago?

Parent and teenager

Read these Scripture passages, then discuss the questions that follow:
Isaiah 9:1-7
Matthew 28:1-20
Mark 1:21-22
Mark 15:21-39
Luke 1:26-33

■ What do these passages tell us about Jesus, the person?
■ What is the most surprising aspect of Jesus' life?
■ What one thing do you wish you better understood about Jesus?
■ How can we develop a closer relationship with Jesus today?
■ How can we celebrate what Jesus has done for us? (Brainstorm several ideas and plan to do one or two of them in the coming weeks.)

Pray together, thanking God for the gift of Jesus.

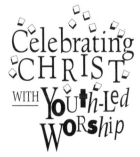

LESSON 2

Jesus, the Master Teacher

Though the church has celebrations for the events surrounding Jesus' birth, death, and resurrection, we rarely get an opportunity to celebrate Jesus' gift for teaching. This lesson will give kids an opportunity to celebrate the incredible messages Jesus taught during his three-year earthly teaching ministry.

LESSON AIM

Teenagers will lead the congregation in celebrating Jesus' teaching ministry.

OBJECTIVES

Students will
■ learn how Jesus taught with authority;
■ explore Jesus' teachings;
■ plan a celebration of Jesus, the teacher; and
■ lead the congregation in a celebration of Jesus, the teacher.

BIBLE BASIS

MARK 1:21-22

Look up the following key Bible passage. Then read the background paragraphs to see how the passage relates to your teenagers. This Scripture will be explored during the Bible study portion of this lesson.

Mark 1:21-22 describes how the people were amazed by Jesus' teaching ability.

While much is said in church about "big" events in Jesus' life, such as his healing abilities or his ultimate sacrifice on the cross, we don't often hear about Jesus' teaching skill. The Jews were amazed at Jesus' teaching ability because he taught "as one with authority," unlike the other teachers of the law. When we look at Jesus the teacher, we learn about the person of Jesus as much as we learn about the message he's teaching.

The further we explore Jesus' teaching ministry, the more we realize that Jesus was passionate about making people think about their faith. Jesus didn't always teach in the expected ways of the time but often chose to leave interpretation up to the disciples. While this frustrated the disciples (and many Christians today as we read the Scriptures), Jesus knew that they'd learn more from the exploration and discovery of the issues than from a pat answer.

Teenagers have pretty strong opinions about good and bad teachers; they've likely had their share of both. Jesus' teaching skill can remind kids that Jesus did more than die for our sins; he also taught his disciples (and us) how to live. Once teenagers begin to struggle with Jesus' teaching (as the disciples did), they'll learn more about walking with Christ and grow closer to him.

THIS LESSON AT A GLANCE

Section	Minutes	What Students Will Do	Supplies
Introduction	up to 10	**Teachers**—Talk about teachers who made an impact on them and why.	
Bible Study	up to 10	**As One With Authority**—Read Mark 1:21-22 and other passages and explore Jesus' role as teacher.	Bibles, paper, pencils
Project Work	up to 30	**Celebrating Jesus, the Master Teacher**—Prepare for and invite church members to participate in the celebration of Jesus' teaching ministry.	"Celebration Plan—Week Two" handouts (p. 16), pencils, celebration supplies (as determined by the celebration plan)
	up to 15	**Coming Soon**—Plan the coming week's celebration activity.	"Celebration Plan—Week Three" handouts (p. 23), pencils
Closing	up to 10	**Pop Quiz**—Complete a quiz affirming each other's abilities.	Paper, pencils, tape

The Lesson

Teachers

(up to 10 minutes)

Welcome students to the class. Say: **Today, in our second week of this course on celebrating Christ, we're going to prepare and present a celebration of Jesus, the master teacher.**

Open with prayer. Welcome visitors and class members who weren't here last week. Have a volunteer explain what the class is doing in this course.

Form groups of no more than four. Have the person in each group who looks most like you begin by telling about his or her favorite teacher and why he or she liked that teacher. Continue with the person to the right and allow no more than one minute for each person to speak.

Then ask the following questions and have kids discuss them in their groups. After they finish their discussions, invite

INTRODUCTION

volunteers to tell the class what they came up with. Ask:

■ **What were the common traits of your favorite teachers?** (They cared; they had a sense of humor; they knew what they were talking about.)

■ **What makes a teacher great?** (Knowledge; concern for students.)

Say: **A good teacher must care for his or her students—and be willing to challenge them. Jesus was more than just a good teacher—he was a master teacher. Before we begin work on today's celebration, let's explore Jesus' teaching ability and some of the great lessons he taught his disciples—and us.**

Table Talk Follow-Up

If you sent the "Table Talk' handout (p. 17) to parents last week, discuss students' reactions to the activity. Ask volunteers to share what they learned from the discussion with their parents.

As One With Authority
(up to 10 minutes)

Form groups of no more than four and pass out paper and pencils. Assign each group one of the following Scripture passages: Mark 1:21-22; John 3:1-2; 7:16-17; and 14:23-24. Then have kids each choose one of the following roles: reader (who will read aloud the passage), reporter (who will report the group's findings to the class), recorder (who will record the group's thoughts), and encourager (who will make sure each person contributes to the conversation).

Say: **In your group read and explore your assigned passage. See what you can determine about Jesus' role as teacher from this passage. You may want to search the surrounding verses to discover more about the context of the passage. Have your recorder make notes of your findings so your reporter can share the results with the class.**

After five minutes have reporters share their groups' findings with the rest of the class. Then ask:

■ **What do these passages tell us about Jesus' teaching ability?** (He taught with authority; people listened when he taught.)

■ **What can we learn about Jesus from the way he taught?** (He wanted to make people think; he was passionate about his message.)

Ask volunteers to tell the class which of Jesus' teachings they most remember or were most affected by. For example, someone might say, "Jesus' message about wealth hit home for me because I usually think money is the key to everything" or "Jesus' message that we're to be like children makes a lot of sense to me."

Say: **The goal of today's lesson is to create a celebration of Jesus' teachings and teaching ability. As we prepare this celebration, let's be thankful for Jesus' powerful lessons. And let's go from this celebration into a deeper study of Jesus' message so we can grow closer to him.**

Celebrating Jesus, the Master Teacher

(up to 30 minutes)

Say: **Let's prepare today's celebration.**

Review last week's decisions about today's celebration. You'll need the "Celebration Plan—Week Two" handouts (p. 16) from last week. If you've already determined how you'll celebrate Jesus, the master teacher, move right into the preparation time. Be prepared to help track down needed supplies.

If you didn't have time to complete the planning for this week's celebration activities, form groups of no more than six and have them complete the first three steps in the "Celebration Plan—Week Two" handout.

Have groups each explain their best celebration idea to the class. As before, you may then choose to vote on one idea or have groups do different ideas. If you choose more than one idea, form groups to do each idea (and complete steps four and five on the handout). If you choose to do only one idea, form small groups of no more than four to brainstorm the details of the idea (steps four and five on the handout). Then have those groups pool their ideas and choose the best way to proceed.

After determining which celebration students want to do, help them choose what they'll do to help make the celebration a success. Refer to the "Responsibilities" box on the "Celebration Plan—Week Two" handout to help kids think about different ways to be involved in the celebration.

When kids have each chosen a responsibility for the celebration, have them prepare for it. To help things go smoothly, assign a leader for each area of responsibility required by the celebration.

If kids need to track down supplies, send them out in small groups, but be sure kids return to your classroom in time to make plans for the coming week's celebration (you'll need up to 15 minutes for this) and for the closing activity (another 10 minutes).

Coming Soon

(up to 15 minutes)

When kids are done preparing for their celebration, form groups of no more than six to brainstorm ideas for next week's celebration activity. Have groups use the "Celebration Plan—Week Three" handout (p. 23) to spark new ideas on the theme of Jesus, our Savior. Encourage kids to vary their celebrations so church members won't know what to expect. For

Teacher Tip

If you're meeting outside of the regular Christian education hour, plan to lead this celebration before, during, or after the next worship service.

Teacher Tip

If your group chooses one large celebration, you may want to form smaller groups of no more than four or five to take on specific responsibilities for the celebration. For example, some kids might want to create a banner, while others might be happier doing a skit in front of the church.

example, this celebration may be more serious because of the subject matter. Kids will want to focus on Jesus' death and resurrection, and what those events mean for each person individually.

After about five or 10 minutes, have groups report what they came up with. Then determine which ideas you'll actually use. If kids need to prepare for the coming week's celebration outside of class time, determine what things they must do. For example, if your celebration requires food, kids would need volunteers to bring food.

If you don't have time to finish the plan for next week's celebration, that's OK. You can use the first part of next week's class to finalize your planning.

Collect the "Celebration Plan—Week Three" handouts to use during next week's lesson. Kids will begin next week's lesson by reviewing their plans for the day's celebration.

CLOSING

Pop Quiz

(up to 10 minutes)

Say: **Since our theme today is teaching, we're going to have a pop quiz to close our lesson time.**

Give each person a sheet of paper and a pencil. Have kids write a column of numbers on the paper from one to the total number of students in your class. Then have kids form a circle and number off.

Say: **Before we celebrate Christ's wonderful teaching abilities, let's celebrate each other. Each number on your paper represents the person in this circle with that number. Here's the question you must answer for each person in class: "What's one ability this person has that I really admire?" The only rule is that your comments must be sincere and positive.**

Have kids complete their quizzes, then tape them to a wall in the room. Close with prayer, then allow kids to wander around and read the comments on the papers before beginning final preparations for today's celebration. Alert the pastoral staff of the celebration ideas you'll be using.

Make a note of any preparations you'll need to do in the coming week for next week's celebration.

If You Still Have Time...

Teacher, Teacher—Form groups of no more than four, and give each group a Bible and a Bible concordance. Have kids look up the word "teacher" and its variations, and explore all the passages about teaching. Have groups share their results.

Teach Me—Form groups of no more than four and have each group choose one of Jesus' messages from the gospels to teach to the other groups. Have each group determine the most effective way to teach that message and then teach the other groups. Discuss how teaching methods affect the way people receive the message.

Use this as a guide for choosing and preparing your celebration activity for this week's theme of celebrating Jesus, our Savior. (Read Mark 15:21-39 and 16:1-6.) For more writing room, use the other side of this handout.

Step 1—

Brainstorm tons of celebration ideas about Jesus, our Savior. Use the "Idea Sparks" below to get you going. The celebration must involve everyone in the group (or the class) and must be do-able with easily available supplies (ask your teacher about available supplies). List your ideas on the back of this handout.

Step 2—

OK, you've thought of lots of ideas. Now choose your favorite. This is the one idea you'll expand further with specific plans, so choose wisely. Describe that idea briefly below:

Step 3—

This celebration's most important goal is for people to discover the personal significance of Jesus' death and resurrection. How well does your idea meet this goal? (If you have a hard time answering this question, you may need to rethink your celebration idea.) Write down why your idea really meets this goal. Wait for further instructions from your teacher.

Responsibilities

Behind the scenes:
- drawing
- coloring
- creating posters
- writing slogans
- collecting supplies
- organizing prop creation
- doing publicity
- soliciting volunteers

In the public eye:
- singing
- speaking
- performing a skit
- leading the congregation
- making announcements

Step 4—

So you're ready to plan a specific celebration? Think about what kinds of responsibilities people will have. Refer to the "Responsibilities" in the box for suggestions. Then list who's responsible for what. Write on the back of your handout, if necessary.

Step 5—

How long will this celebration be? When will you present it? Remember, the celebration must involve the congregation in some way. List details on the back of this handout.

IDEA SPARKS

Here are a few starter ideas to get the brainstorming going for this week's celebration:
- Create personalized "Jesus Died for Me" pins to give to each congregation member.
- Lead a time of silent prayer, thanking God for sending Jesus to die for our sins.
- Build an altar and have people pause at the altar to praise God for sending Jesus as our Savior.
- Form groups of no more than three and go around the congregation, gathering 10 or more people together and leading them in singing "Jesus Saves" or another hymn about Jesus, our Savior.
- Use craft supplies to create a symbol of Jesus' death on the cross and present it to the church during worship.
- Prepare a reading or skit that begins in a somber mood (representing Jesus' death), then explodes into a confetti-filled celebration (representing Jesus' resurrection).

Jesus, Our Savior

The most important aspect of Jesus' life is, ironically, his death (and subsequent resurrection). Understanding that Jesus died for "me" is one of the most powerful realizations of our faith walk. The project for this week explores the exciting reality of Jesus as our Savior.

LESSON AIM

Teenagers will lead the congregation in celebrating Jesus' role as Savior.

OBJECTIVES

Students will
- learn what it means that Jesus died for our sins,
- explore the salvation Jesus' death and resurrection brings,
- plan a celebration of Jesus as the Savior, and
- lead the congregation in a celebration of Jesus, our Savior.

BIBLE BASIS

MARK 15:21-39; 16: 1-6

Look up the following key Bible passages. Then read the background paragraphs to see how the passages relate to your teenagers. These Scriptures will be explored during the Bible study portion of today's lesson.

Mark 15:21-39 and **16:1-6** describe Jesus' crucifixion and resurrection.

Through these familiar, dramatic passages, our lives take on new meaning. Jesus didn't die in vain or just for a select few—he died for me, for you, for everyone. Jesus' death and resurrection are at the very center of our faith.

When we begin to realize the personal nature of Jesus' death on the cross, we're often stunned that God would send his Son to die for such sinful people. Yet we can celebrate that God cared so much for us that he did this great act. Just as God was glorified through his own Son's death and resurrection, we can sing God's praises and celebrate Jesus, our Savior.

Section	Minutes	What Students Will Do	Supplies
Introduction	up to 10	**Easter Memories**—Guess each other's Easter memories.	Life Savers
Bible Study	up to 10	**Save Me!**—Read Mark 15:21-39 and 16:1-6 and explore what it means that Jesus is our Savior.	Bibles, 3×5 cards, pencils, tape
Project Work	up to 30	**Celebrating Jesus, Our Savior**—Prepare for and invite church members to participate in the celebration of the fact that Jesus died for them.	"Celebration Plan—Week Three" handouts (p. 23), pencils, celebration supplies (as determined by the celebration plan)
	up to 15	**Coming Soon**—Plan the coming week's celebration activity.	"Celebration Plan—Week Four" handouts (p. 29), pencils
Closing	up to 10	**Thank You, Jesus**—Thank Jesus for dying for their sins.	

The Lesson

Easter Memories

(up to 10 minutes)

Welcome students to the class. Say: **Today, in our third week of this course on celebrating Christ, we're going to prepare and present a celebration of Jesus, our Savior.**

Open with prayer. Welcome visitors and class members who weren't here last week. Have a volunteer explain what the class is doing in this course.

Form groups of no more than three. Starting with the person in each group whose birthday is closest to Easter, have kids take turns telling a favorite Easter-season memory. Ask kids to keep their memories brief so others can repeat them.

Then have kids in each group take someone else's memory and tell it to the class as if it were his or her memory. Have the class attempt to guess whose memory they're being told. Continue until each person's memory has been guessed. Ask:

■ **What is it about the Easter season that makes it important to our faith?** (Jesus died and rose again; Jesus' death on the cross paved the way for us to know God.)

Say: **So far we've explored how Jesus' birth brought**

INTRODUCTION

great hope to the world. We've discovered how Jesus, the master teacher, helps us grow in faith. But the most important aspect of Christ's life is probably his death—and resurrection. Today we'll explore what it means that Jesus is our Savior, then prepare a celebration of this aspect of Christ's life for the whole congregation to enjoy. Each of you may have a Life Saver candy now to get you in the mind-set of discussing Jesus, our "Ultimate Life Savior!"

Hand out Life Saver candies.

Save Me!

(up to 10 minutes)

Form groups of no more than five. (You can divide up according to Life Saver colors.) Have groups each read Mark 15:21-39 and 16:1-6. Then have kids discuss the following questions in their groups:

■ **What's the significance of these events for Christians today?** (Jesus died for our sins; if Jesus didn't rise from the dead our faith would be meaningless.)

■ **What does the word "Savior" mean to you?** (Jesus saved us from death; Jesus took our place on the cross.)

Distribute 3×5 cards, pencils, and tape. Have groups brainstorm a list of the world's problems; for example, starvation in Third World countries, the nation's deficit, the threat of nuclear war, racism, poverty, the homeless, and so on. Have groups list each problem on a separate 3×5 card. Make sure groups have at least as many problems as they have group members.

Have group members each take one world problem and tape it to another group member as they say, "(Name), I hereby lay all the blame on you for (the problem). It's all your fault."

Then ask kids each to tell their groups how it felt being blamed for the world's problems.

Have groups discuss the following questions, then report their insights to the class:

■ **How did you feel when you were blamed for something you didn't do?** (Overwhelmed; I didn't take it seriously.)

■ **How does this experience help you understand Jesus' role as Savior?** (Jesus took on our sins and suffered our pain; we didn't deserve to have Jesus die for us; even though we're sinful people, Jesus loved us enough to take on our sin.)

Have someone read aloud or quote John 3:16. Ask:

■ **In light of this message, how must we respond to Jesus' death on the cross?** (We must celebrate God's love for us; we must ask forgiveness for our sins.)

■ **How does the church celebrate the eternal life that Jesus' death on the cross brings?** (Through Easter services; by praising God.)

■ **How does if feel to know that Jesus died specifically for you?** (I can't fathom it; I feel loved; I don't know how to feel.)

Say: **Jesus' death and resurrection gave each of us the opportunity to once again be in a real relationship with God. While there are many mysteries we may never understand about Jesus' role as Savior, we can celebrate the one truth we can all experience—that Jesus' death and resurrection was for you, and me, and each person in our church, and our world.**

Let's celebrate that fact!

Celebrating Jesus, Our Savior

(up to 30 minutes)

Review last week's decisions about today's celebration. You'll need the "Celebration Plan—Week Three" handouts (p. 23) from last week. If you've already determined how you'll celebrate the theme Jesus, our Savior, move right into the preparation time. Be prepared to help track down needed supplies.

If you didn't have time to complete the planning for this week's celebration activities, form groups of no more than six and have them complete the first three steps in the "Celebration Plan—Week Three" handout.

Then have groups each explain their best celebration idea to the class. As before, you may then choose to vote on one idea or have groups do different ideas. If you choose more than one idea, form groups to do each idea (and complete steps four and five on the handout). If you choose to do only one idea, form small groups of no more than four to brainstorm the details of the idea (steps four and five on the handout). Then have those groups pool their ideas and choose the best way to proceed.

After determining which celebration kids want to do, help them choose what they'll do to make the celebration a success. Refer to the "Responsibilities" box on the "Celebration Plan—Week Three" handout to help kids think about different ways to be involved in the celebration.

When kids have each chosen a responsibility for the celebration, have them prepare for it. To help things go smoothly, assign a leader for each area of responsibility required by the celebration.

If kids need to track down supplies, send them out in small groups, but be sure kids return to your classroom in time to make plans for the final week's celebration (you'll need 10 to 15 minutes for this) and for the closing activity (another 10 minutes).

Coming Soon

(up to 15 minutes)

When kids are prepared for their celebration, form groups of no more than six to brainstorm ideas for next week's celebration activity. Have groups use the "Celebration Plan—Week Four" handout (p. 29) to spark ideas on the theme Jesus will return.

For this last week of the course, have kid create some kind of

Teacher Tip

If you're meeting outside of the regular Christian education hour, plan to lead this celebration before, during, or after the next worship service.

Teacher Tip

If your class chooses one large celebration, you may want to form smaller groups of no more than four or five to take on specific responsibilities for the celebration. For example, some kids might want to act out a scene, while others might be happier creating props.

lasting reminder of the fourth week's theme. This could be a banner, a poem, a mural, or another similar idea. The reminder can be a small part of the celebration or the main focus. Ideas for this kind of lasting reminder are included in the "Idea Sparks" section of the "Celebration Plan—Week Four" handout.

After about five or 10 minutes, have groups report what they came up with. Then determine which ideas you'll use. If kids need to prepare for the coming week's celebration outside of class time, determine what they must do. For example, if your celebration requires food, kids would need volunteers to bring food.

If you don't have time to plan for next week's celebration, that's OK. You can use the first part of next week's class to finalize your planning. Collect the "Celebration Plan—Week Four" handouts for use in next week's lesson. Kids will begin next week's lesson by reviewing their plans for the day's celebration.

CLOSING

Thank You, Jesus
(up to 10 minutes)

Say: **Today's celebration is a special one. As we celebrate Jesus' death and resurrection, we're celebrating the aspect of Jesus' life that has brought us together in faith. Let's prepare for this celebration by spending a few minutes in prayer. In your prayers, focus on thanking Jesus for being willing to die for us.**

In preparation for today's celebration activity, have kids form circles of no more than five and spend three or four minutes in prayer. Kids may choose how they want to pray in their groups. Some may choose to have one person pray, others may want each person to pray, and still others may choose silent prayer.

When time is up, say "amen." Before directing kids to make the final preparations for today's celebration, have kids each take a few minutes to tell each person in their group one way Jesus' life shines through him or her. As they affirm one another, have them "draw" an invisible cross on the person's hand.

Alert the pastoral staff of the celebration ideas you'll be using. Make a note of any preparations you'll need to do in the coming week for next week's celebration.

If You Still Have Time...

John 3:16—Form groups of no more than four and have each group come up with a creative way to share the message of this passage through a skit, song, pantomime, or any other method. Then have kids perform their version of the familiar passage. Encourage kids to be just as creative when they tell others about Jesus, their Savior.

Further Exploration—Have kids read Exodus 15:2; Acts 4:12; and Ephesians 2:8-10 and discuss what the verses say about eternal life. Have kids form research groups to interview other church members about what eternal life means to them. Then have groups share their findings with the class.

CELEBRATION PLAN—WEEK FOUR

Use this as a guide for choosing and preparing your celebration activity for this week's celebration theme, Jesus will return. (Read Matthew 28:20b; John 14:1-3; and 1 Thessalonians 4:13-18.) For more writing room, use the other side of this handout.

Step 1—

Brainstorm tons of celebration ideas about Jesus' return. Use the "Idea Sparks" below to get you going. The celebration must involve everyone in the group (or the class) and must be do-able with easily available supplies (ask your teacher about available supplies).

NOTE: As a part of this celebration, create a lasting reminder of the theme that the church can display for years to come. See the "Lasting Reminders" section in the "Idea Sparks" below. List your ideas on the back of this handout.

Step 2—

OK, you've thought of lots of ideas. Now choose your favorite. This is the one idea you'll expand further with specific plans, so choose wisely. Describe that idea briefly below:

Step 3—

This celebration's most important goal is for people to get excited about Jesus' return. How well does your idea meet this goal? (If you have a hard time answering this question, you may need to rethink your celebration idea.) Write down why your idea really meets this goal. Wait for further instructions from your teacher.

Step 4—

So you're ready to plan a specific celebration? Think about what kinds of responsibilities people will have. Refer to the "Responsibilities" box for suggestions. Then list who's responsible for what. Write on the back of your handout, if necessary.

Step 5—

How long will this celebration be? When will you present it? Remember, the celebration must involve the congregation in some way. List details on the back of this handout.

Responsibilities

Behind the scenes:
- drawing
- coloring
- creating posters
- writing slogans
- collecting supplies
- organizing prop creation
- doing publicity
- soliciting volunteers

In the public eye:
- singing
- speaking
- performing a skit
- leading the congregation
- making announcements

IDEA SPARKS

Here are a few starter ideas to get the brainstorming going for this week's celebration:
- Hold a "coming-soon" party based on the theme of Christ's return.
- Prepare a song praising God that Christ lives and will return (write new lyrics to a familiar hymn).
- Make banners celebrating that Christ lives today.
- Serve Now and Later candies.
- Shine flashlights in a darkened room on a ceiling banner that celebrates Jesus' second coming.

- Hold a wedding reception celebrating the ultimate marriage of Christ to the church at the second coming.

Lasting Reminders

- Create a cloth banner with the words, "Jesus Is Coming Again" that can hang in the front of the church.
- Use a craft supplies to create a sculpture based on the theme, Jesus lives.
- Combine the themes from all four weeks and create a mural depicting what Jesus has done for us.
- Record a song celebrating Jesus' second coming and play this for the church every week as people enter or leave worship services.

Jesus Will Return

Christians are part of a continuing story—a story that places its hope on the return of Christ. As this course comes to a close, teenagers will discover that Jesus' story doesn't end with his resurrection. Through this lesson, kids will celebrate that Jesus lives today and the promise that Jesus will soon return.

LESSON AIM

Teenagers will lead the congregation in celebrating the promise of Jesus' return.

OBJECTIVES

Students will
- learn what it means to hope for something,
- explore the excitement of living expectantly,
- plan a celebration of Jesus' promise to return, and
- lead the congregation in a celebration of the promise of Jesus' return.

BIBLE BASIS

MATTHEW 28:20b
JOHN 14:1-3
1 THESSALONIANS 4:13-18
REVELATION 22:20

Look up the following key Bible passages. Then read the background paragraphs to see how the passages relate to your teenagers. These Scriptures will be explored during the Bible study portion of today's lesson.

In **Matthew 28:20b** Jesus promises that he will always be with us.

In this final verse of Matthew's gospel, we're reminded that Jesus is just as near today as he was in the first century. This is important to understand because our relationship with a living Jesus is the basis for our faith. Knowing that Jesus is always with us gives us strength to face the tough times ahead.

In **John 14:1-3; 1 Thessalonians 4:13-18;** and **Revelation 22:20,** we learn of Jesus' promise to return.

We live in the hope of Jesus' promised return. As we strive to follow Jesus, we're going to face pain and suffering (Jesus never promised an easy life). Yet the hope of Jesus' return can help us discover pure joy in the midst of difficult times.

Section	Minutes	What Students Will Do	Supplies
Introduction	up to 10	**Hopes**—Tell something they hope for.	
Bible Study	up to 10	**The Promise**—Explore Bible passages about the promise of Jesus' return.	Bibles, snack foods
Project Work	up to 35	**Celebrating the Promise of Jesus' Return**—Prepare for and invite church members to participate in the celebration of the fact that Jesus will return.	"Celebration Plan—Week Four" handouts (p. 29), pencils, celebration supplies (as determined by the celebration plan)
	up to 10	**Wrap Up and Review**—Review memories from the past weeks' celebrations.	
Closing	up to 10	**Celebrating Each Other**—Celebrate good things about each other.	Noisemakers

The Lesson

Hopes

(up to 10 minutes)

Welcome students to the class. Say: **Today, in our final week of this course on celebrating Christ, we're going to prepare and present a celebration of Jesus' promise to return.**

Open with prayer. Welcome visitors and class members who weren't here last week. Have a volunteer explain what the class is doing in this course.

Form a circle. Have kids take turns completing the following sentence: "One hope that I have in my life is . . . "

Then have kids find partners who have similar hopes. Have partners discuss the following questions:

■ **Why do you hope for this thing?** (Answers will vary.)

■ **What role does hope play in our lives?** (It keeps us going; it helps us through tough times.)

Say: **Hope is a powerful medicine for tough times. And the hope of Christ's return is one of the driving forces in our faith. This is our final week of this course on celebrating Christ. Today, as we explore the promise of Jesus' return, let's think of ways we can celebrate the promise of Christ's return each day.**

INTRODUCTION

The Promise

(up to 10 minutes)

Begin this activity by promising kids a special treat sometime during the class hour. Tell kids what the treat will be (choose one of their favorites), but don't tell them when they'll get to eat it. Have fun getting kids excited about the coming treat.

Form groups of four. Have kids number off from one to four in their groups. Then send the "ones" to one corner of the room, the "twos" to another, and so on. Assign the following passages to each numbered group: ones, Matthew 28:20b; twos, John 14:1-3; threes, 1 Thessalonians 4:13-18; and fours, Revelation 22:20.

Say: **In your group read your passage and prepare a creative way to present this message to the members of your original group. For example, you might compose a poem, a cheer, or a one-person skit based on the message.**

Allow no more than four minutes for groups to read and prepare their brief presentations. Then have the kids return to their original groups and take turns presenting each Scripture's message in creative ways.

After the presentations ask the following questions. Have kids discuss them in their groups, then tell the class what they discussed. Ask:

■ **How did you feel as you presented this message?** (Excited; nervous; unsure; happy.)

■ **How do these Scripture messages make you feel?** (Happy; excited; hopeful.)

■ **How does Jesus' promise that he'll return affect the way we live our lives today?** (We want to make the right choices; we can look forward to happiness; we need to tell others about Christ.)

Stop the discussion abruptly and bring out the treats for kids. As you serve the treats, ask:

■ **What was it like to suddenly receive the promised treats?** (I was surprised; I liked getting the food.)

■ **How was this experience like or unlike the way you picture Christ's return?** (We'll be surprised; we'll be excited to see Jesus.)

■ **What are ways we can celebrate Jesus' promise in our daily lives?** (We can praise God for Jesus; we can be a part of the church; we can follow Jesus' example in our daily living.)

Say: **The promise of Jesus' return is something worth celebrating. As we continue to celebrate today with these treats, let's also prepare our celebration for the whole church.**

Celebrating the Promise of Jesus' Return

(up to 35 minutes)

Review last week's decisions about today's celebration. You'll need the "Celebration Plan—Week Four" handouts (p. 29) from last week. If you've already determined how you'll celebrate the theme of Jesus' return, move right into the preparation time. Be prepared to help track down needed supplies.

If you didn't have time to complete the planning for this week's celebration activities, form groups of no more than six and have them complete the first three steps in the "Celebration Plan—Week Four" handout.

Then have groups each explain their best celebration idea to the class. As before, you may then choose to vote on one idea or have groups do different ideas. If you choose more than one idea, form groups to do each idea (and complete steps four and five on the handout). If you choose to do only one idea, form small groups of no more than four to brainstorm the details of the idea (steps four and five on the handout). Then have those groups pool their ideas and choose the best way to proceed.

After determining which celebration kids want to do, help them choose what they'll do to make the celebration a success. Refer to the "Responsibilities" box on the "Celebration Plan—Week Four" handout to help kids think about different ways to be involved in the celebration.

When kids have each chosen a responsibility for the celebration, have them prepare for it. To help things go smoothly, assign a leader for each area of responsibility required by the celebration.

Remember that this week you want kids to prepare a lasting reminder of the celebration that the church can keep for years to come. This can be a small part of the celebration or the main focus. Refer to the "Idea Sparks" section of the "Celebration Plan—Week Four" handout for a few lasting-reminder ideas.

If kids need to track down supplies, send them out in small groups, but be sure kids return to your classroom in time to review the past four weeks of class (you'll need 5 to 10 minutes for this) and for the closing activity (another 10 minutes).

Wrap Up and Review

(up to 10 minutes)

Form a circle of chairs and have kids stand in front of their chairs. Ask the following questions one at a time. Have a volunteer answer the question, then sit down. If kids have nothing new to add to this person's answer, they may also sit. Continue until everyone is seated. Then have kids stand again for each of the other questions. Ask:

■ **What has impacted you most about this course?**

■ **What memory from this course will stay with you for a long time?**

■ **What have you learned about celebrating Christ that you can use in your daily lives?**

■ **How does the hope of Christ's return affect your life?**

Thank kids for their honest responses. Then have them gather for the closing activity before making final preparations for today's celebration.

Teacher Tip

If you're meeting outside of the regular Christian education hour, plan to lead this celebration before, during, or after the next worship service.

Teacher Tip

If your class chooses one large celebration, you may want to form smaller groups of no more than four or five to take on specific responsibilities for the celebration. For example, some kids might want to create decorations, while others might be happier leading cheers in front of the church.

Teacher Tip

Since this is the final week of the celebrating Christ course, kids won't need to spend any time preparing for next week. Use all the time you have left to make this the biggest celebration yet.

Celebrating Each Other

(up to 10 minutes)

Say: **For the past four weeks we've been working together and celebrating different aspects of Jesus' life. Whenever people work together on a project, they learn about each other as well as the project. So to close our class time, we're going to celebrate some of the good things we discovered about each other.**

Hand out noisemakers to everyone, then form a circle. Beginning with the person on your left, have each person take a turn standing in the middle of the circle while others call out positive things about that person.

Encourage kids to call out good things they saw that person do or positive traits they saw that person express during the past four weeks of class. For example, someone might say, "I really appreciated your patience" or "Your artistic talent made our banner great."

After a few positive comments have been spoken, make noise with your noisemaker and have kids join you in the mini-celebration. Continue until each person (including you!) has been recognized for his or her special qualities.

Then have one final noisy celebration of each other's gifts, talents, and abilities before closing. Have volunteers close with prayer.

When kids have finished praying, say "amen" and help them with final preparations for today's celebration. Alert the pastoral staff of the celebration ideas you'll be using.

After the celebration today, thank class members individually for their good ideas and participation. Look at the "Party Pleasers" section in the "Bonus Ideas" chapter (p. 35) for ways to celebrate your teenagers' accomplishments.

If You Still Have Time...

Revelation Exploration—Have kids read Revelation 22:1-21 and explore what this chapter says about Jesus' return and the coming kingdom.

If Jesus Came Today...—Have kids form groups of no more than four and discuss how they'd respond if they knew Jesus was returning in 24 hours. Encourage kids to tell how their daily actions would change during that time. Ask:

■ How can we learn from the changes we'd make in this circumstance to make our daily lives more pleasing to God?

■ How can we live each day as if Christ will return?

Bonus Ideas

Bonus Scriptures—The lessons focus on a select few Scripture passages, but if you'd like to incorporate more Bible readings into a lesson, here are some suggestions:

- Matthew 1:18-25 (Jesus is born.)
- Matthew 3:1-17 (Jesus is baptized.)
- John 5:19-47 (Jesus asserts his authority.)
- John 13:13 (Jesus is teacher and Lord.)
- Acts 16:29-34 (Belief in Jesus brings eternal life.)
- Philippians 2:5-11 (Jesus humbles himself before God.)

Exploring the Gospels—Have kids explore the life of Christ through a study of one or more of the gospels. Have kids form small groups of no more than five for the studies and meet once a week outside of regular church activities to read and discuss the passages. How about a short-term "breakfast bunch"? Or lead kids through *The Gospel of John* or *Who Is Jesus?* Active Bible Curriculum courses (Group Publishing) to give them a better understanding of Christ's life.

On the Road to Jerusalem—Have kids read the Gospel of Mark and create an around-the-room mural depicting the events in Jesus' life, from the moment he gathers his disciples until his death and resurrection. Have kids meet for a few weeks to read the book and create the huge mural. When it's complete, have an unveiling ceremony and invite the whole church to attend.

Awaiting Jesus' Return—Have kids get permission to paint the ceiling of your youth room or Christian education room. Then have kids explore passages about Jesus' second coming and paint these scenes or Bible passages on the ceiling of the room. Use a white coat of paint (or two, if necessary) as a primer for the ceiling, then let kids use a variety of colors to paint their masterpiece. You'll need scaffolding for kids to do the painting (expect plenty of paint spills).

This ceiling painting can symbolize the return of Christ and serve as a constant reminder for kids to live Christlike lives.

Taking the Celebration on the Road—Have kids choose their favorite celebration activity from the four-week course (or create a new one) and prepare a version of the celebration to take to nursing homes, shut-ins, or other places willing to allow a party celebrating Christ.

MEETINGS AND MORE

PARTY PLEASERS

Thanks for Teachers—Supply apples, toothpicks, construction paper, markers, and tape. Have students decorate mini thank-you flags for the apples. Then deliver the apples to all the teachers at the church.

Growing Closer to Christ—After kids complete the course, have them continue their study of Jesus' life on their own or in pairs. Have kids explore the gospels and keep daily or weekly journals of their discoveries. Then, every month or so, meet with the kids who've kept journals. Have them share their insights.

Christlike Awards—Have kids explore the life of Christ further and determine what characteristics they consider Christlike. Then have kids prepare awards out of easy-to-find craft items. Have them choose congregation members to receive the awards. For example, kids might award a "servant's heart" award to someone who volunteers time helping the elderly in your church.

Kids could make this an annual event or give an award out whenever they think of someone who deserves it.

A Celebration of Celebrations—Plan a party for kids after the fourth week of this course to celebrate their accomplishments. During the party (which should include plenty of their favorite foods and games) award prizes to kids for their good ideas and participation in the celebrations. Take time to recall stories of what happened during their planning and what responses the congregation had.

For added meaning, have people from the congregation attend the party and give their thanks to kids for their work on the celebrations.

Surprise!—Give kids a surprise they won't soon forget by arranging to have the congregation throw a big party for the teenagers following the fourth celebration.

Have congregation members prepare food and secretly decorate the room in the church where the party will be held. Then, following the worship service (and the kids' celebration), have the congregation members lead the kids back to the party. Have them thank the students for making Christ the focus of their church for the past four weeks.

RETREAT IDEA

A Big Idea—Hold a retreat for the purpose of planning a huge celebration event involving the whole church on the theme Jesus, our friend (or another topic chosen by the kids).

During the retreat have kids brainstorm ways to make the celebration an unforgettable experience for the entire congregation. For example, kids might create a giant banner, attach it to helium balloons, and fly it outside the church (check local sign ordinances and make sure the area is safe if kids choose an activity such as this).

Or kids might spend the entire weekend preparing handmade celebration booklets for each congregation member. The booklets could contain kids' favorite Scripture passages, illustrations, and original poems or writings about Jesus' life.

CURRICULUM REORDER—TOP PRIORITY

Order now to prepare for your upcoming Sunday school classes, youth ministry meetings, and weekend retreats! Each book includes all teacher and student materials—plus photocopiable handouts—for any size class . . . for just $8.99 each!

FOR SENIOR HIGH:

1 & 2 Corinthians: Christian Discipleship,
ISBN 1-55945-230-7

Angels, Demons, Miracles & Prayer, ISBN 1-55945-235-8

Changing the World, ISBN 1-55945-236-6

Christians in a Non-Christian World,
ISBN 1-55945-224-2

Christlike Leadership, ISBN 1-55945-231-5

Communicating With Friends, ISBN 1-55945-228-5

Counterfeit Religions, ISBN 1-55945-207-2

Dating Decisions, ISBN 1-55945-215-3

Dealing With Life's Pressures, ISBN 1-55945-232-3

Deciphering Jesus' Parables, ISBN 1-55945-237-4

Exodus: Following God, ISBN 1-55945-226-9

Exploring Ethical Issues, ISBN 1-55945-225-0

Faith for Tough Times, ISBN 1-55945-216-1

Forgiveness, ISBN 1-55945-223-4

Getting Along With Parents, ISBN 1-55945-202-1

Getting Along With Your Family, ISBN 1-55945-233-1

The Gospel of John: Jesus' Teachings,
ISBN 1-55945-208-0

Hazardous to Your Health: AIDS, Steroids & Eating Disorders, ISBN 1-55945-200-5

Is Marriage in Your Future?, ISBN 1-55945-203-X

Jesus' Death & Resurrection, ISBN 1-55945-211-0

The Joy of Serving, ISBN 1-55945-210-2

Knowing God's Will, ISBN 1-55945-205-6

Life After High School, ISBN 1-55945-220-X

Making Good Decisions, ISBN 1-55945-209-9

Money: A Christian Perspective, ISBN 1-55945-212-9

Movies, Music, TV & Me, ISBN 1-55945-213-7

Overcoming Insecurities, ISBN 1-55945-221-8

Psalms, ISBN 1-55945-234-X

Real People, Real Faith: Amy Grant, Joni Eareckson Tada, Dave Dravecky, Terry Anderson, ISBN 1-55945-238-2

Responding to Injustice, ISBN 1-55945-214-5

Revelation, ISBN 1-55945-229-3

School Struggles, ISBN 1-55945-201-3

Sex: A Christian Perspective, ISBN 1-55945-206-4

Today's Lessons From Yesterday's Prophets,
ISBN 1-55945-227-7

Turning Depression Upside Down, ISBN 1-55945-135-1

What Is the Church?, ISBN 1-55945-222-6

Who Is God?, ISBN 1-55945-218-8

Who Is Jesus?, ISBN 1-55945-219-6

Who Is the Holy Spirit?, ISBN 1-55945-217-X

Your Life as a Disciple, ISBN 1-55945-204-8

FOR JUNIOR HIGH/MIDDLE SCHOOL:

Accepting Others: Beyond Barriers & Stereotypes,
ISBN 1-55945-126-2

Advice to Young Christians: Exploring Paul's Letters,
ISBN 1-55945-146-7

Applying the Bible to Life, ISBN 1-55945-116-5

Becoming Responsible, ISBN 1-55945-109-2

Bible Heroes: Joseph, Esther, Mary & Peter,
ISBN 1-55945-137-8

Boosting Self-Esteem, ISBN 1-55945-100-9

Building Better Friendships, ISBN 1-55945-138-6

Can Christians Have Fun?, ISBN 1-55945-134-3

Caring for God's Creation, ISBN 1-55945-121-1

Christmas: A Fresh Look, ISBN 1-55945-124-6

Competition, ISBN 1-55945-133-5

Dealing With Death, ISBN 1-55945-112-2

Dealing With Disappointment, ISBN 1-55945-139-4

Doing Your Best, ISBN 1-55945-142-4

Drugs & Drinking, ISBN 1-55945-118-1

Evil and the Occult, ISBN 1-55945-102-5

Genesis: The Beginnings, ISBN 1-55945-111-4

Guys & Girls: Understanding Each Other,
ISBN 1-55945-110-6

Handling Conflict, ISBN 1-55945-125-4

Heaven & Hell, ISBN 1-55945-131-9

Is God Unfair?, ISBN 1-55945-108-4

Love or Infatuation?, ISBN 1-55945-128-9

Making Parents Proud, ISBN 1-55945-107-6

Making the Most of School, ISBN 1-55945-113-0

Materialism, ISBN 1-55945-130-0

The Miracle of Easter, ISBN 1-55945-143-2

Miracles!, ISBN 1-55945-117-3

Peace & War, ISBN 1-55945-123-8

Peer Pressure, ISBN 1-55945-103-3

Prayer, ISBN 1-55945-104-1

Reaching Out to a Hurting World, ISBN 1-55945-140-8

Sermon on the Mount, ISBN 1-55945-129-7

Suicide: The Silent Epidemic, ISBN 1-55945-145-9

Telling Your Friends About Christ, ISBN 1-55945-114-9

The Ten Commandments, ISBN 1-55945-127-0

Today's Faith Heroes: Madeline Manning Mims, Michael W. Smith, Mother Teresa, Bruce Olson, ISBN 1-55945-141-6

Today's Media: Choosing Wisely, ISBN 1-55945-144-0

Today's Music: Good or Bad?, ISBN 1-55945-101-7

What Is God's Purpose for Me?, ISBN 1-55945-132-7

What's a Christian?, ISBN 1-55945-105-X

Order today from your local Christian bookstore, or write: Group Publishing, Box 485, Loveland, CO 80539. For mail orders, please add postage/handling of $4 for orders up to $15, $5 for orders of $15.01+. Colorado residents add 3% sales tax.

MORE PROGRAMMING IDEAS FOR YOUR ACTIVE GROUP...

DO IT! ACTIVE LEARNING IN YOUTH MINISTRY

Thom and Joani Schultz

Discover the keys to teaching creative faith-building lessons that teenagers look forward to...and remember for a lifetime. You'll learn how to design simple, fun programs that will help your kids...

- build community,

- develop communication skills,

- relate better to others,

- experience what it's really like to be a Christian,

...and apply the Bible to their daily challenges. Plus, you'll get 24 ready-to-use active-learning exercises complete with debriefing questions and Bible application. For example, your kids will...

- learn the importance of teamwork and the value of each team member by juggling six different objects as a group,

- experience community and God's grace using a doughnut,

- grow more sensitive to others' needs by acting out Matthew 25:31-46

...just to name a few. And the practical index of over 30 active-learning resources will make your planning easier.

ISBN 0-931529-94-8

DEVOTIONS FOR YOUTH GROUPS ON THE GO

Dan and Cindy Hansen

Now it's easy to turn every youth group trip into an opportunity for spiritual growth for your kids. This resource gives you 52 easy-to-prepare devotions that teach meaningful spiritual lessons using the experiences of your group's favorite outings. You'll get devotions perfect for everything from amusement parks, to choir trips, to miniature golf, to the zoo. Your kids will gain new insights from the Bible as they...

- discuss how many "strikes" God gives us—after enjoying a game of softball,

- experience the hardship of Jesus' temptation in the wilderness—on a camping trip,

- understand the disciples' relief when Jesus calmed the storm—while white-water rafting, even

...learn to trust God's will when bad weather cancels an event or the bus breaks down!

Plus, the handy topical listing makes your planning easy.

ISBN 1-55945-075-4

PUT FAITH INTO ACTION WITH...

Want to try something different with your 7th—12th grade classes? Group's NEW Projects With a Purpose™ for Youth Ministry offers four-week courses that really get kids into their faith. Each Project With a Purpose course gives you tools to facilitate a project that will provide a direct, purposeful learning experience. Teenagers will discover something significant about their faith while learning the importance of working together, sharing one another's troubles, and supporting one another in love...plus they'll have lots of fun!

Each lesson-complete leaders book offers four sessions. Use for Sunday school classes, midweek, home Bible studies, youth groups, retreats, or any time you want to help teenagers discover more about their faith.

These easy-to-teach lessons will help your teenagers learn deep insights about their faith! Your kids will learn more about each other. They'll practice the life skill of working together. And you'll be rewarded with the knowledge that you're providing a life-changing, faith-building experience for your church's teenagers.

Titles Available:

Acting Out Jesus' Parables	1-55945-147-5
Serving Your Neighbors	1-55945-406-7
Checking Your Church's Pulse	1-55945-408-3
Sharing Your Faith Without Fear	1-55945-409-1
Teaching Teenagers to Pray	1-55945-407-5
Teenagers Teaching Children	1-55945-405-9
Videotaping Your Church Members' Faith Stories	1-55945-239-0